HIEROGLYPHIC
Coloring Book

With warmest thanks to Professor David Silverman for his many
suggestions and corrections during the making of this book, and
to Susan Wageman and Cynthia Stretch for typesetting and
proofreading the final manuscript.

– G. Schar

Published by the Grand Lodge of the English Language, Jurisdiction, AMORC, Inc., San Jose, California

ISBN 0-912057-57-2

P/N 507440

READING EGYPTIAN HIEROGLYPHS

The picture writing of ancient Egypt is the most beautiful ever created. Living close to the land, the Egyptians modelled the lovely symbols of their written language after the living things, the earth and the objects of daily use in the Nile Valley. A farmer's hoe, a stonecutter's chisel, a flower, a bird -- almost anything might be chosen to write their words, and the number of things they chose was enormous. This coloring book contains only a sampling of the many hundreds of different hieroglyphs.

In its simplest form, picture writing refers directly to the object or action intended. For example, a picture of a vulture would simply mean "vulture," or a pair of striding legs would mean "walk." However, a language based entirely on individual pictures to represent the many thousands of words in the vocabulary would be very cumbersome. Secondly, there are many words that cannot be easily expressed in pictures.

Realizing this problem, the ancient Egyptians developed a way to simplify the writing of words without having to memorize countless thousands of different symbols. By phonetic borrowing, they created an **alphabet** of hieroglyphs representing all of the sounds in their language, each of which represents a single consonantal sound and a few semi-vowels (see the top panel on the inside front cover). To list a few, the sound ≡ was derived from their word for vulture , the sound **p** was derived from their word for mat , the sound **r** was derived from their word for mouth , and so on. This list contained all of the necessary signs needed to **spell** words. Almost all Egyptian words contain one or more of these alphabetic **sound-signs.**

The Egyptian language contained more than one hundred additional sound-signs that expressed combinations of two and three consonants (see the bottom panel on the inside front cover). These additional signs were almost always combined with alphabetic signs that aided in their pronunciation. Alphabetic signs used in this manner are called **phonetic complements** and they may express part or all of the sound value of combination signs. They may be placed after the combination sign, as in , or before the sign, as in , usually for reasons of space. The word for bulti-fish has them both before and after the two-consonant sign .

Along with the sound-signs, the Egyptian language employed hundreds of other hieroglyphs that were essential to the correct reading of words. These are called **sense-signs** (see the inside of the back cover). Having no sound value, they were always placed at the **end** of the spelled word and helped to indicate its meaning. The Egyptian language, as with other languages, contained words that were spelled with the same sound-signs and yet had entirely different meanings. For example, the words for **obelisk** and **eye injury** were both spelled with the same sound-signs, . To distinguish the sense of the meaning of one word from the other, the sense-signs and were needed. Thus, obelisk was written as and eye injury was written as .

TRANSLITERATION AND PRONUNCIATION

On transliteration. Vowels were not written in Egyptian words. Signs such as 🦅 , ⌐ , ⌐ , and 🦆 are weak consonants or semi-vowels. Since the voiced elements are missing in Egyptian spellings, today's standard practice is to indicate or transliterate only the consonants in the words with their equivalents in English letters. Some of these letters have special markings on them to express sounds that are similar to, and yet different from, the letters shown. Among them are **ḥ**, **ḫ**, **ẖ**, **š**, **ḳ**, **ṯ**, and **ḏ**. Two of the sound indicators, ꝫ and ꜥ were created for Egyptian sounds unknown to English.

On Pronunciation. Obviously, in their transliterated form, Egyptian words are unpronounceable. To pronounce the transliterated words in this book, a short **e** has been inserted between the letters. Thus, for example, bnt is written be**ne**t. ꝫ and ꜥ are rendered as "a." The guttural and palatal sounds are written with their closest equivalent to English spelling. Under "pronunciation" in the pages of this book, **ḥ** becomes **h**, **ḫ** becomes **kh**, **ẖ** becomes **ch**, **š** becomes **sh**, **ḳ** becomes **q**, **ṯ** becomes **tch** and **ḏ** becomes **dj**. It must be remembered that these English approximations of pronunciation are purely artificial and may bear little, if any, resemblance to how the ancient Egyptians actually pronounced their words.

GROUPING AND DIRECTION OF WRITING

Where possible, hieroglyphs were written in square or rectangular groups to make them more appealing to the eye. ⬯ instead of ⌁ ⬮ ⌒ . The Egyptians were very much aware of the beauty of their language. When reading these groups, the uppermost sign is read first. In the word for goat, ☥⬮🐐 , the group of signs following ☥ is read from top to bottom and, in this case, left to right, as follows: ☥ + ⌁ + ⬮ + ⌒ + 🐐 . The order of reading is determined by the direction in which the signs face. To determine the direction of reading, find a human or animal figure. The direction it faces points to the beginning of the word. If it faces left, the word begins on the left and reads left to right. The goat faces **towards** the beginning of the word.

The ancient Egyptians usually wrote their words from right to left and only occasionally from left to right. They also wrote both in vertical and horizontal columns. Here are the four possible ways:

(the numbers indicate the order in which the hieroglyphs are to be read)

This coloring book is arranged to be read from left to right, as English is read.

Authors note: To maximize the use of coloring space, many of the hieroglyphs in this book are drawn out of proportion to their accompanying signs. Egyptian tradition kept the signs more uniform in size. Thus, for example, ⌐⌁🔺 , a more correct writing of the word, appears as ⌐🔺 in this book.

Transliteration	Pronunciation	Meaning
ꝫꞀꝫꞀ	AKH AKH	STARS

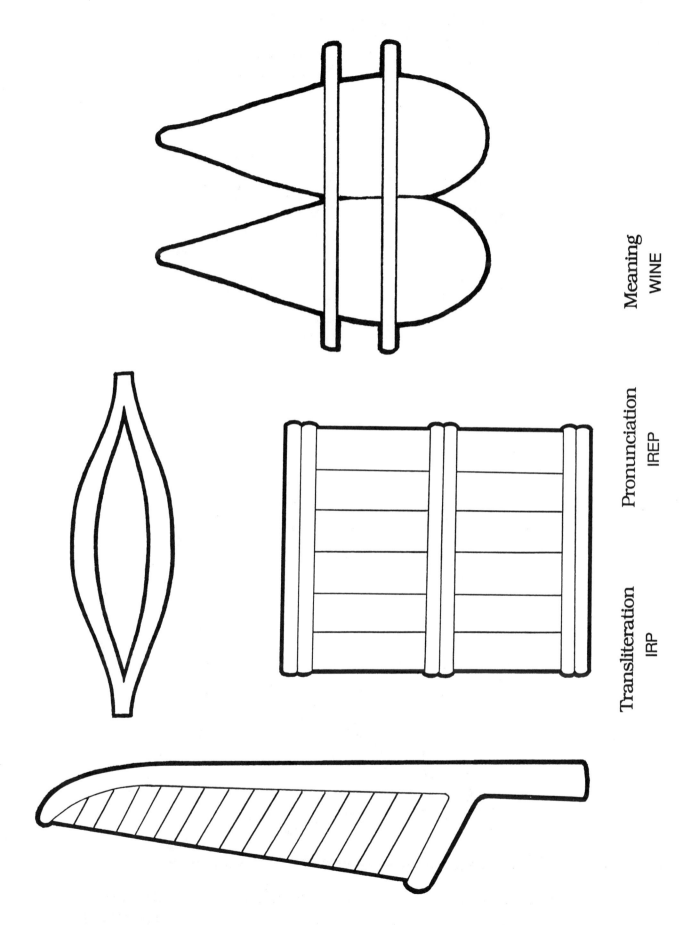

Meaning
WINE

Pronunciation
IREP

Transliteration
IRP

Y

Transliteration	Pronunciation	Meaning
IRY	IRY	COMPANION

Transliteration
ꜥN

Pronunciation
AN

Meaning
BEAUTIFUL

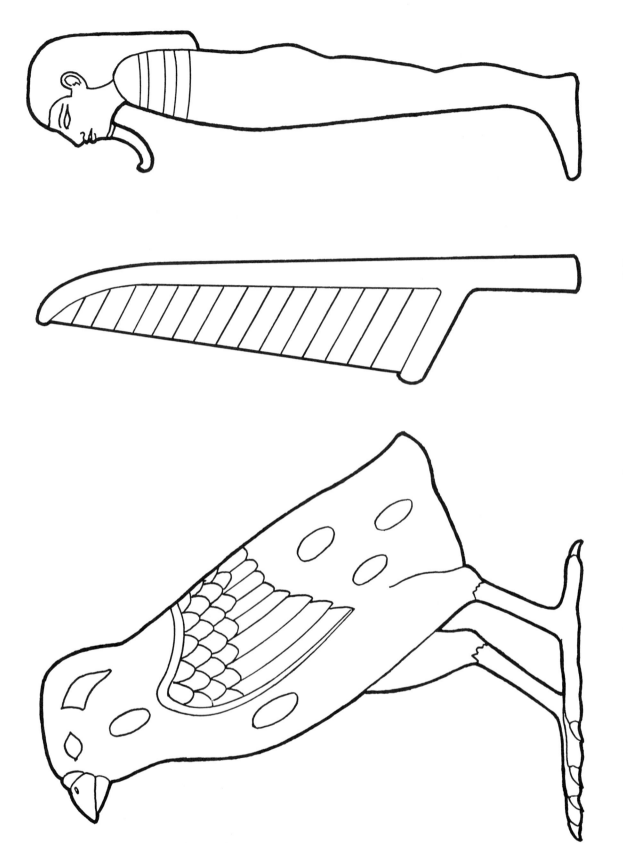

W

Meaning
MUMMY

Pronunciation
WI

Transliteration
WI

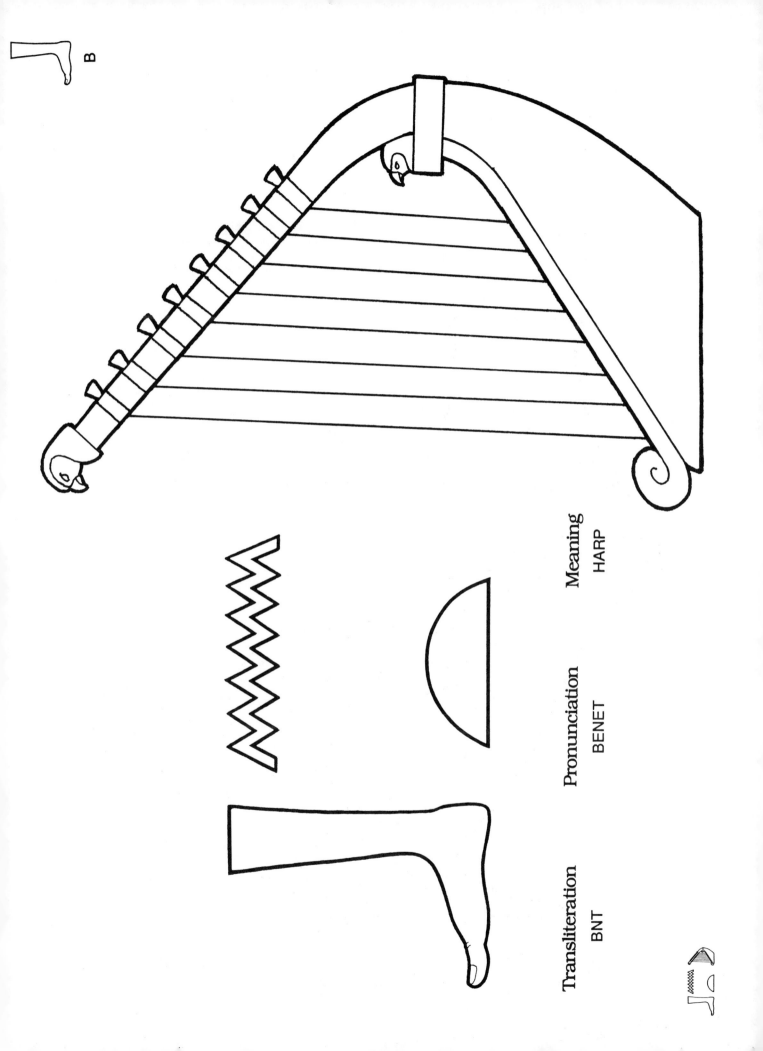

B

Transliteration
BNT

Pronunciation
BENET

Meaning
HARP

P

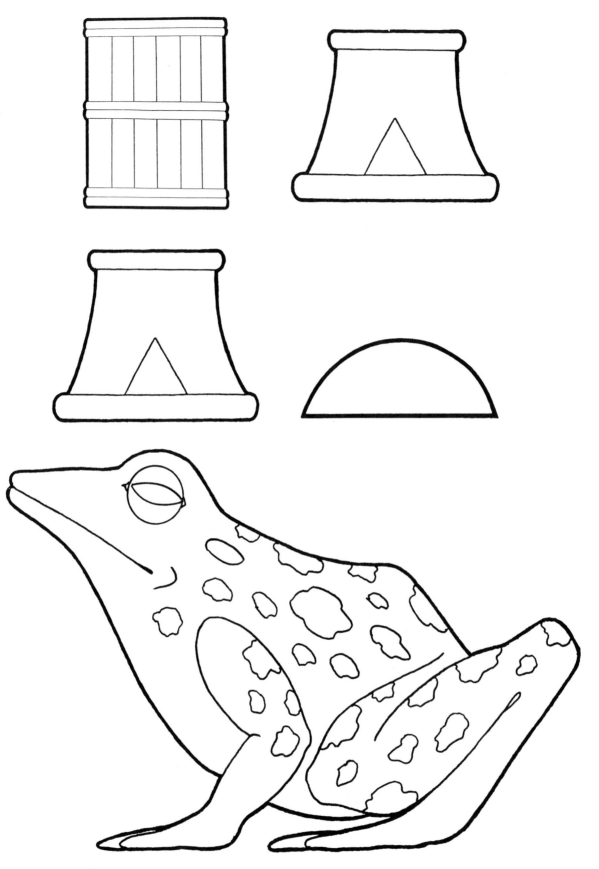

Transliteration	Pronunciation	Meaning
PGGT	PEGEGET	FROG

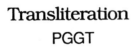

F

Transliteration	Pronunciation	Meaning
FN**I**	FENETCH	SNAKE

M

Transliteration
MSḤ.

Pronunciation
MESEH

Meaning
CROCODILE

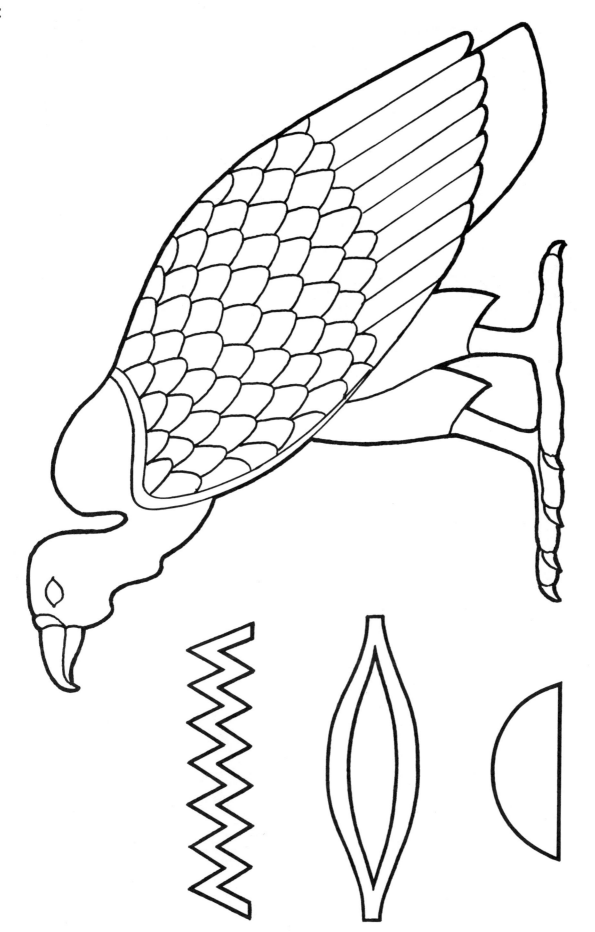

Transliteration
NRT

Pronunciation
NERET

Meaning
VULTURE

R

Transliteration	Pronunciation	Meaning
RNY	RENY	CALF

Transliteration	Pronunciation	Meaning
HBY	HEBY	IBIS

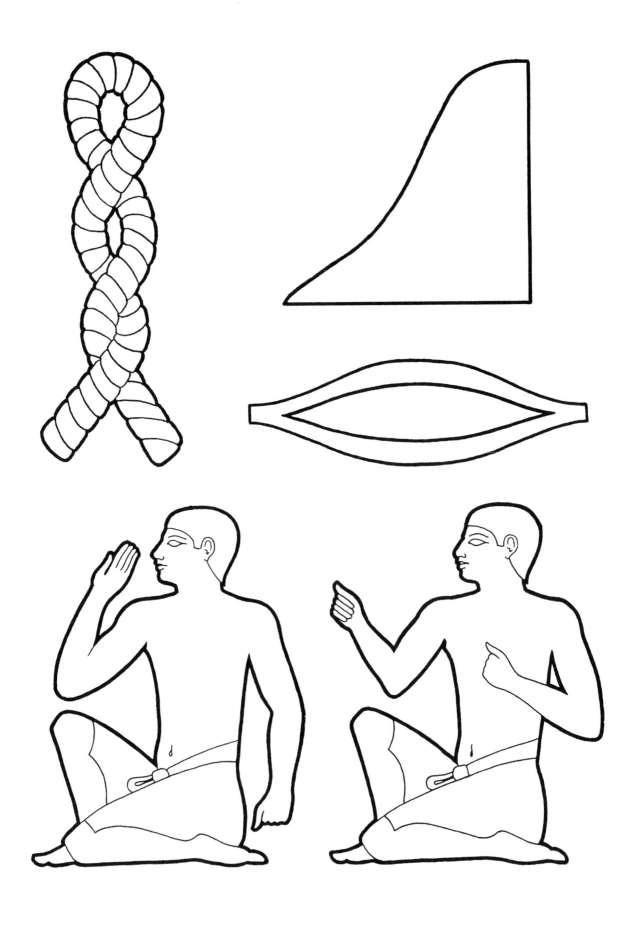

Transliteration	Pronunciation	Meaning
ḤḲR	HEQER	HUNGRY MAN

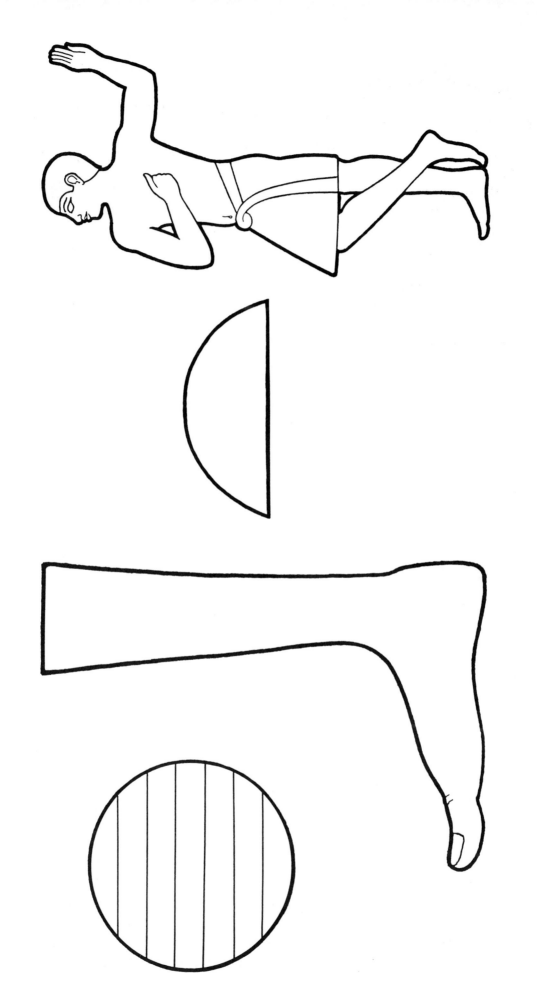

Transliteration
ḪBT

Pronunciation
KHEBET

Meaning
DANCE

Transliteration
ḤT

Pronunciation
CHET

Meaning
PEOPLE

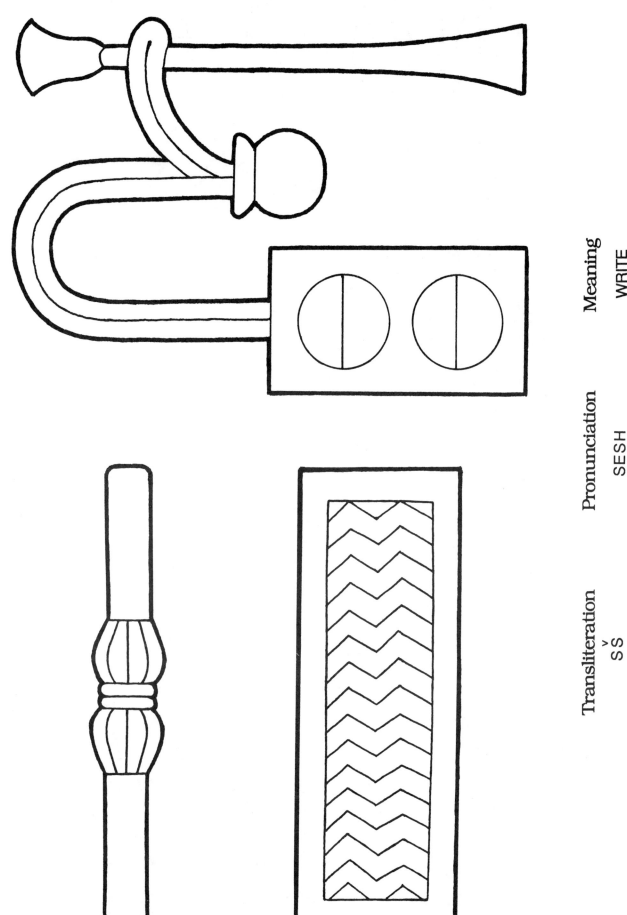

S

Meaning
WRITE

Pronunciation
SESH

Transliteration
SŠ

Transliteration	Pronunciation	Meaning
SSMT	SESEMET	HORSE

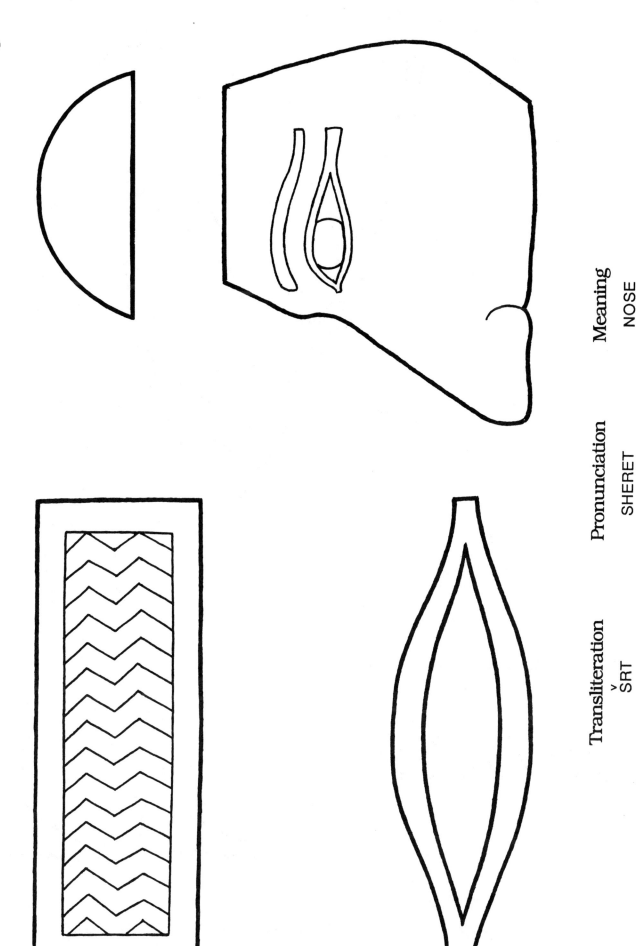

Š

Transliteration
Š́RT

Pronunciation
SHERET

Meaning
NOSE

Transliteration	Pronunciation	Meaning
ḲN[I]	QENI	BRAVE

Transliteration	Pronunciation	Meaning
KKW	KEKU	DARKNESS

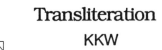

G

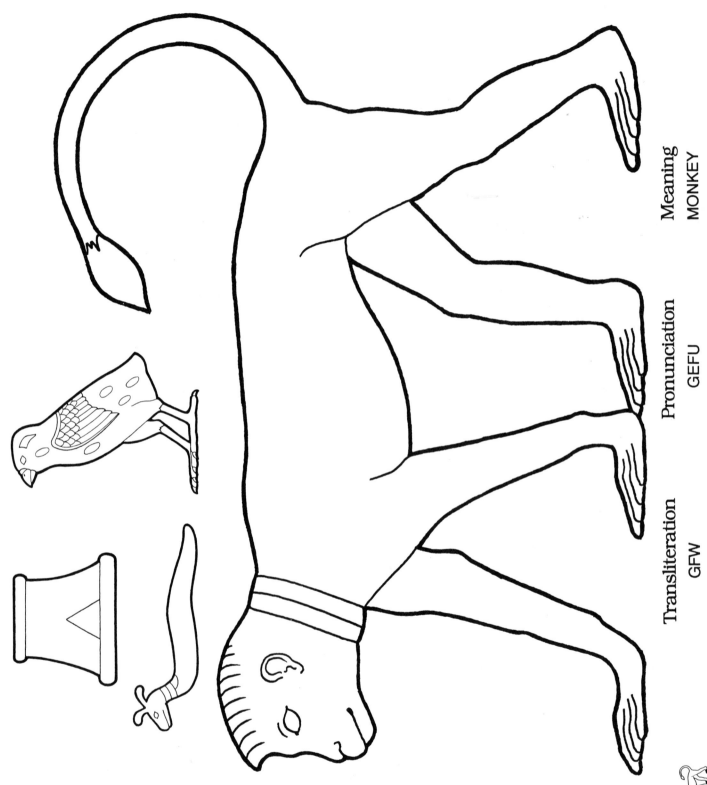

Transliteration
GFW

Pronunciation
GEFU

Meaning
MONKEY

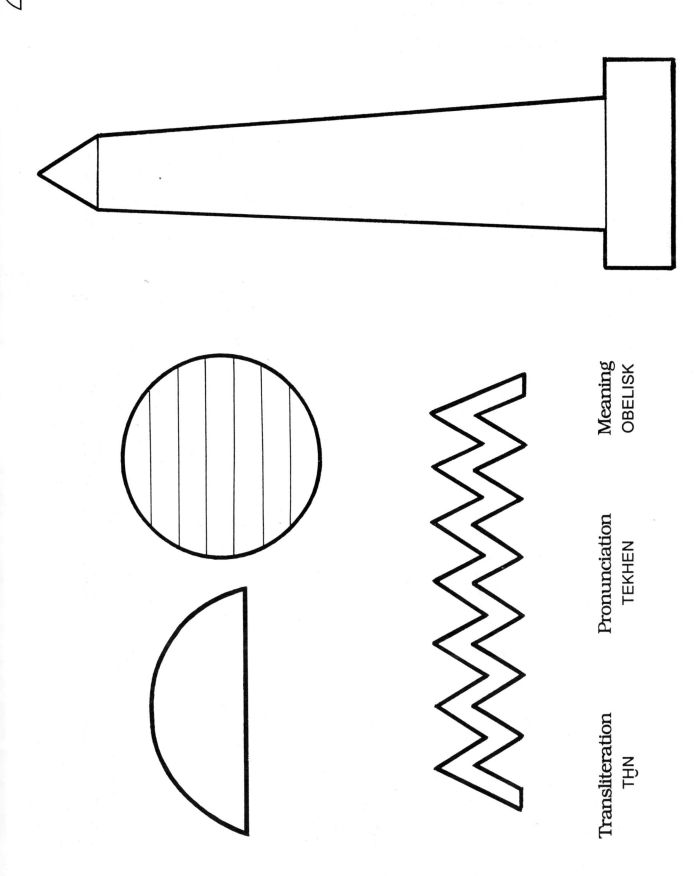

Transliteration
TḪN

Pronunciation
TEKHEN

Meaning
OBELISK

I

Transliteration	Pronunciation	Meaning
ṮSM	TCHESEM	HOUND

D

Transliteration
DB

Pronunciation
DEB

Meaning
HIPPOPOTAMUS

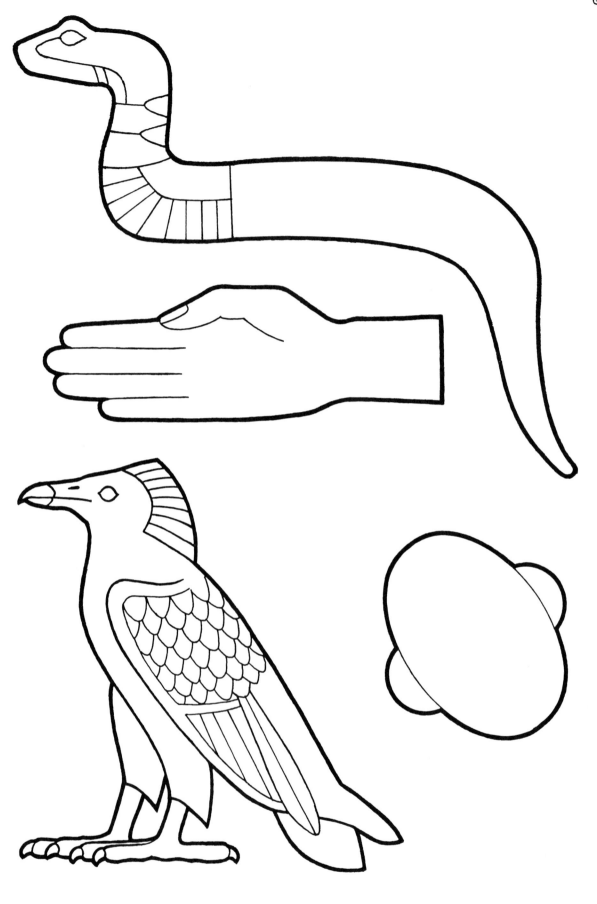

D

Transliteration	Pronunciation	Meaning
ḎḎȝ	DJEDA	FAT

B3

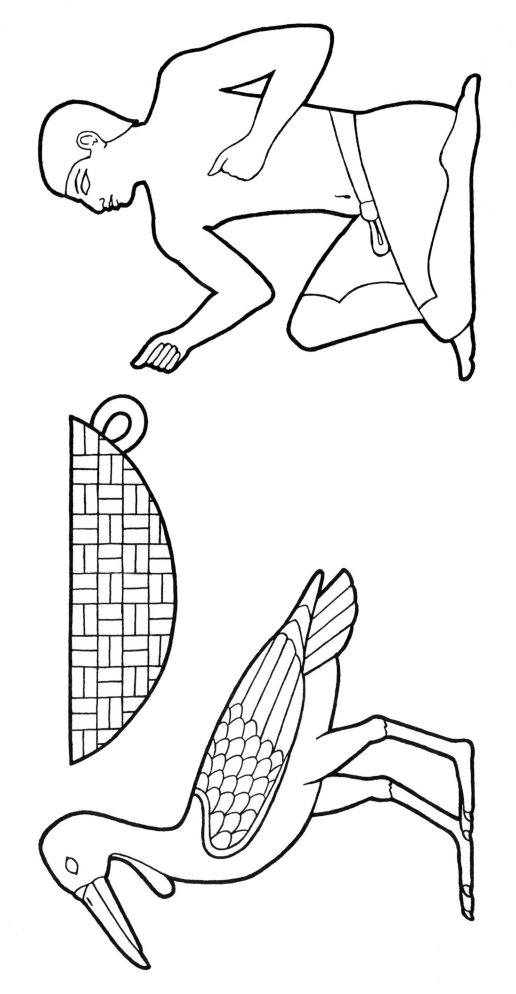

Transliteration
BꝨK

Pronunciation
BAK

Meaning
SERVANT

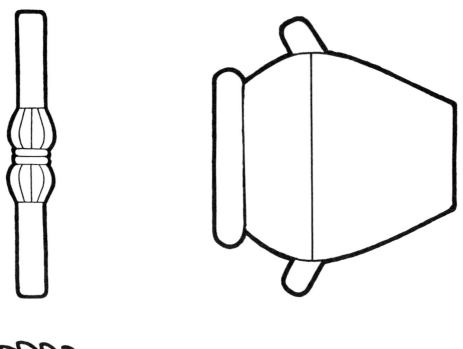

P3

Meaning
WATER JAR

Pronunciation
PAS

Transliteration
P3S

C

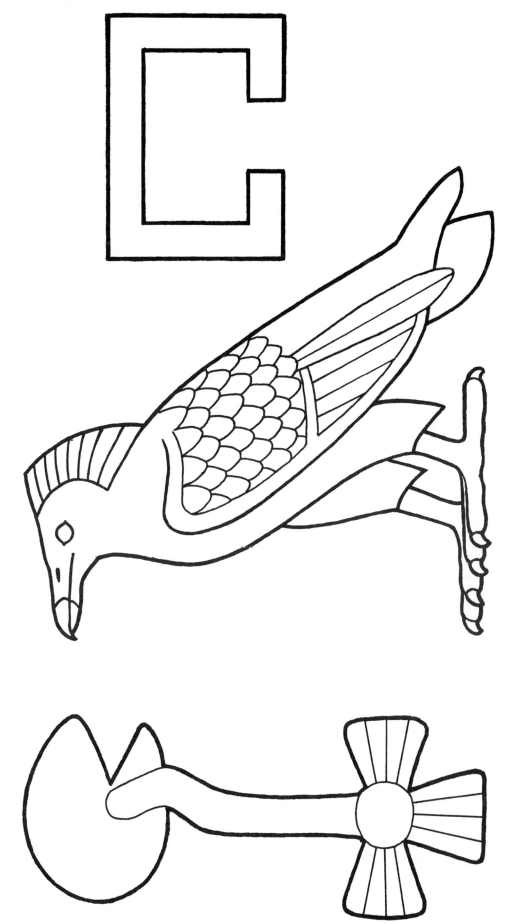

Transliteration
ḫ3

Pronunciation
KHA

Meaning
OFFICE

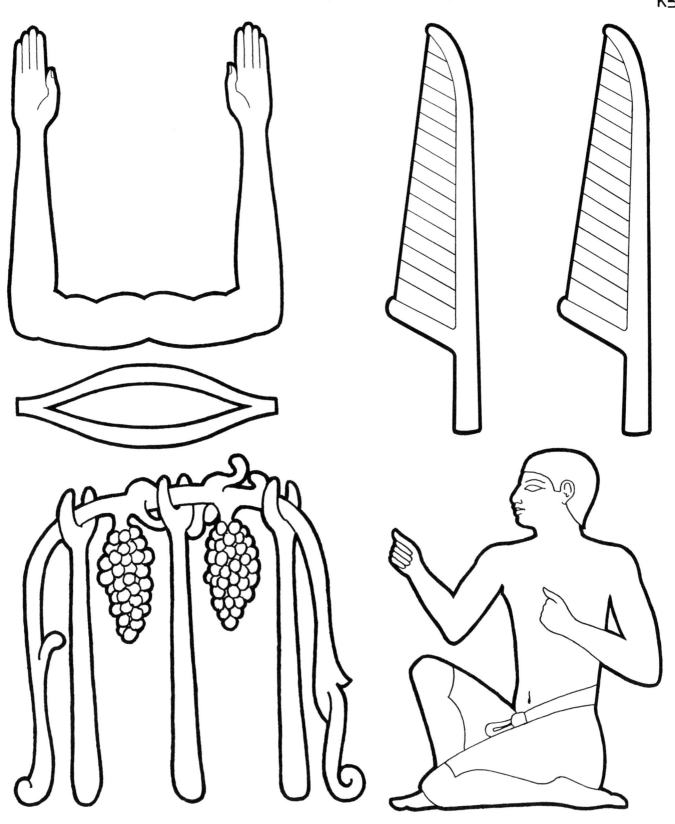

Transliteration	Pronunciation	Meaning
K3RY	KARY	GARDENER

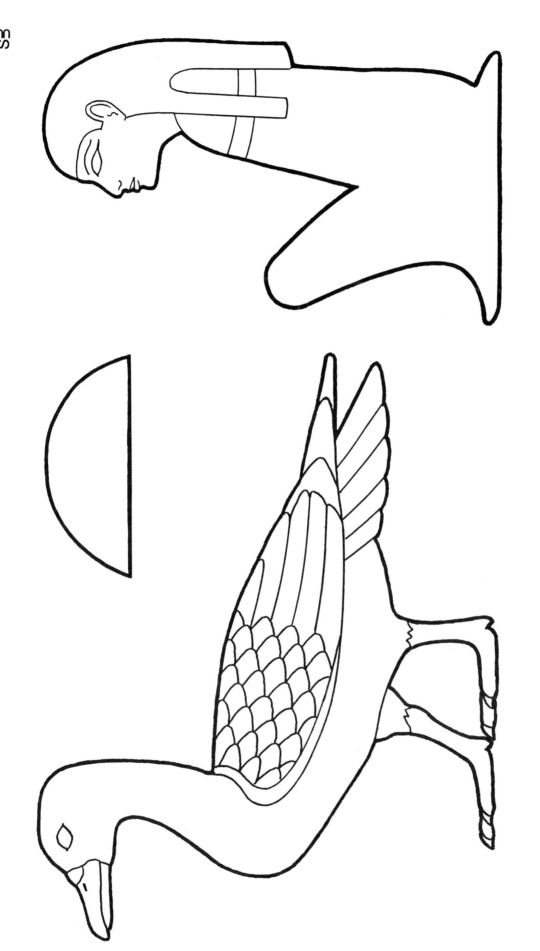

Transliteration
SꜢT

Pronunciation
SAT

Meaning
DAUGHTER

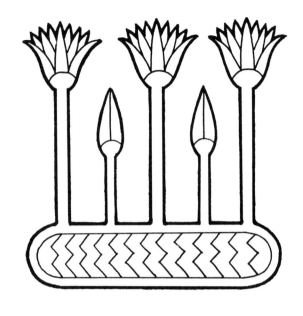

Transliteration	Pronunciation	Meaning
šꜣI	SHAI	PIG

IW

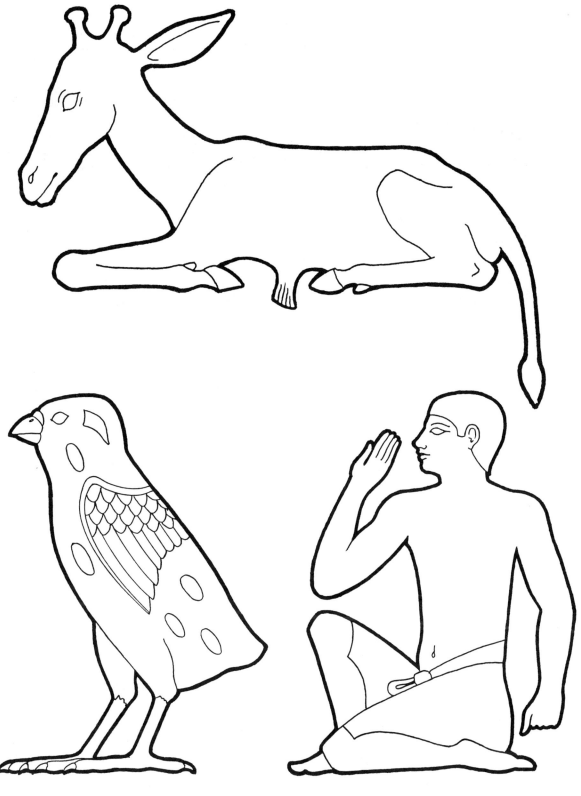

Transliteration	Pronunciation	Meaning
IW	YU	CRY OUT

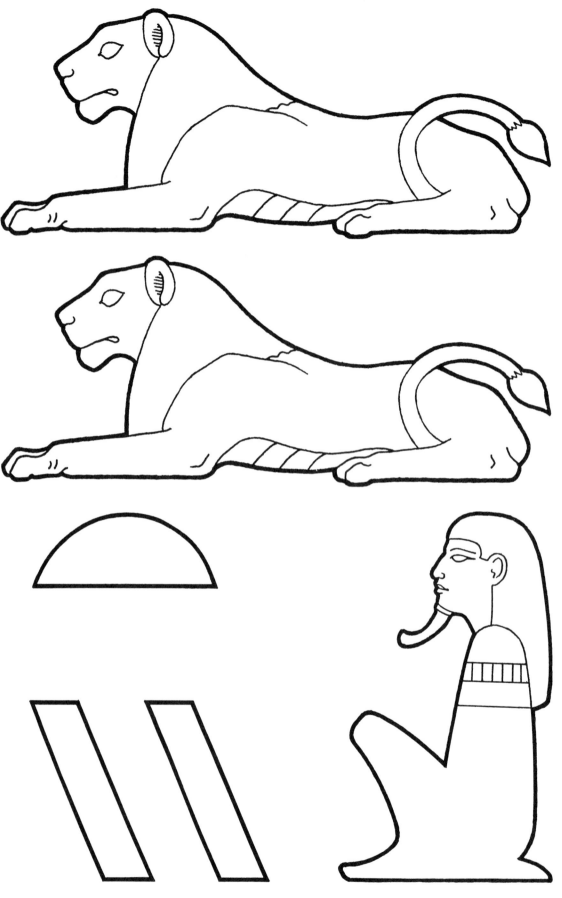

Transliteration	Pronunciation	Meaning
RWTY	RUTY	TWO-LION GOD

IN

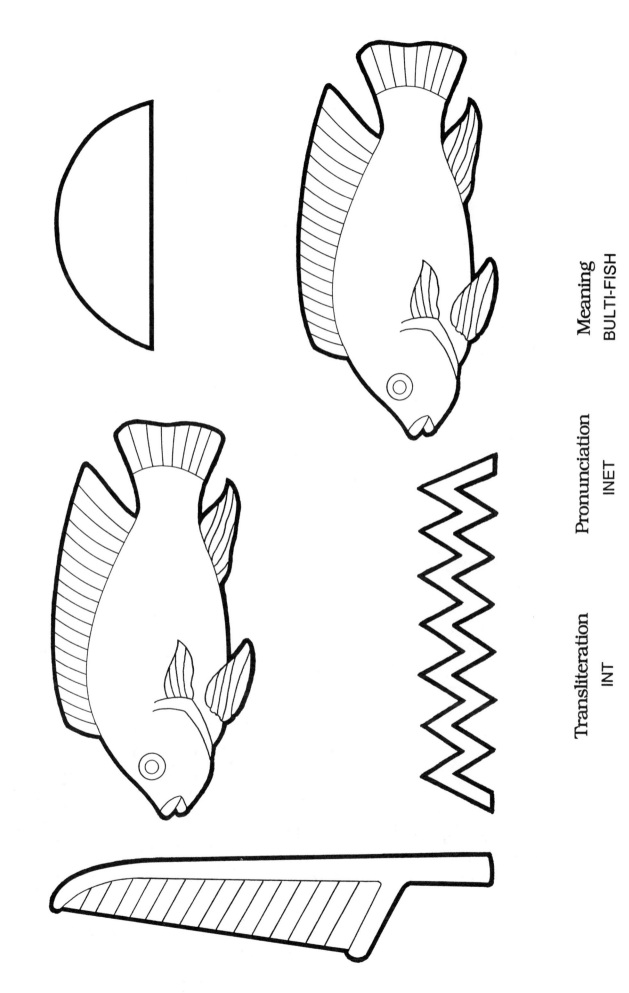

Transliteration
INT

Pronunciation
INET

Meaning
BULTI-FISH

Transliteration	Pronunciation	Meaning
WNM	WENEM	TO EAT

Transliteration	Pronunciation	Meaning
GMḤ	GEMEH	TO LOOK

MI

Transliteration	Pronunciation	Meaning
MIW	MIU	CAT

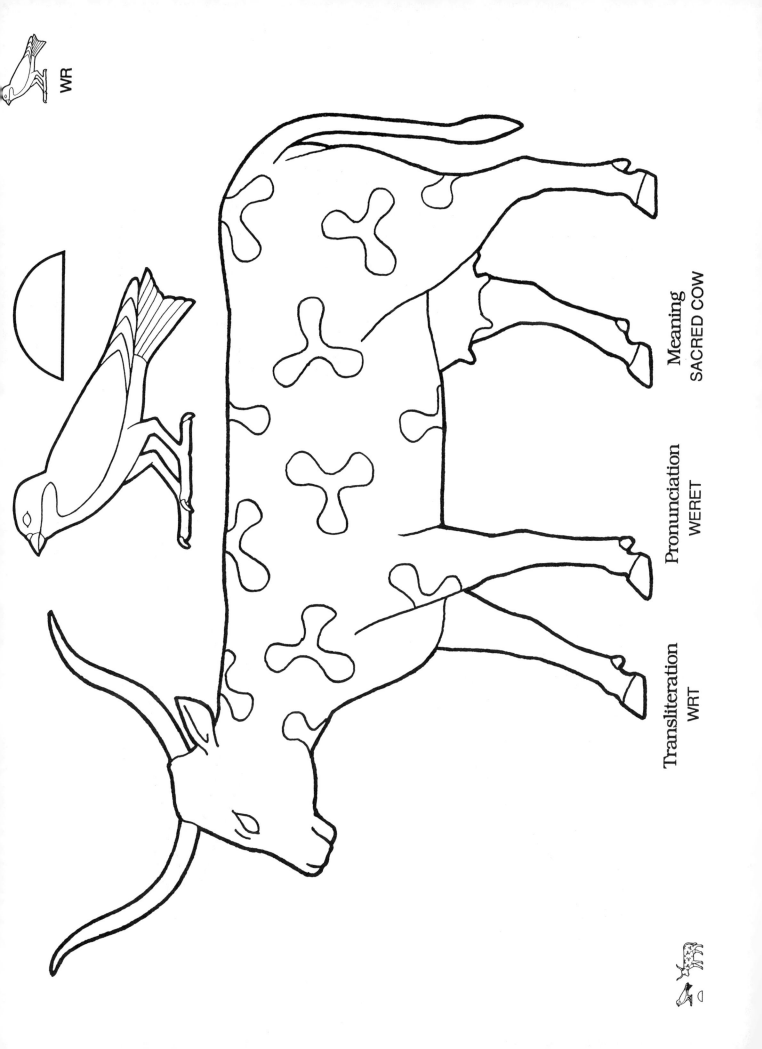

WR

Transliteration
WRT

Pronunciation
WERET

Meaning
SACRED COW

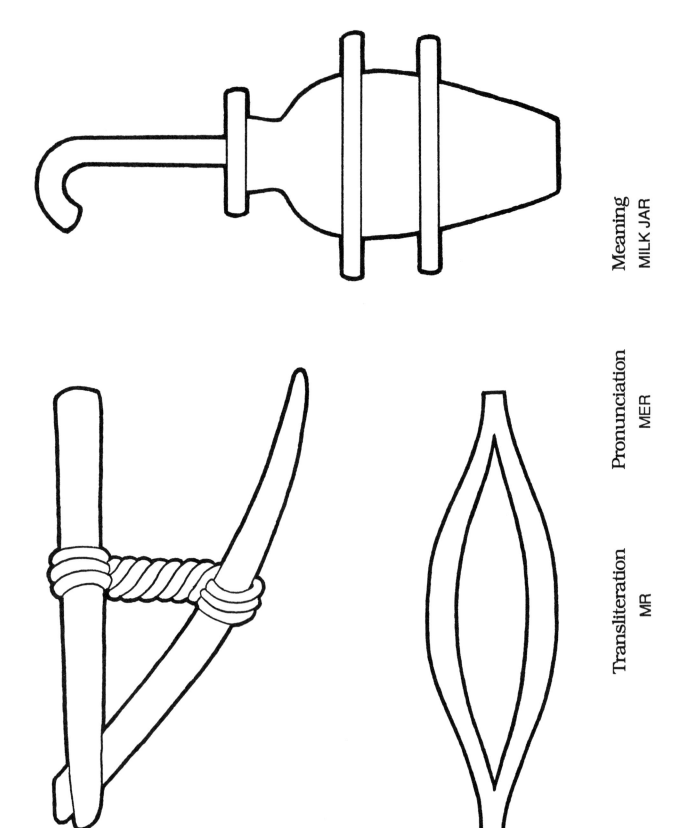

MR

Meaning
MILK JAR

Pronunciation
MER

Transliteration
MR

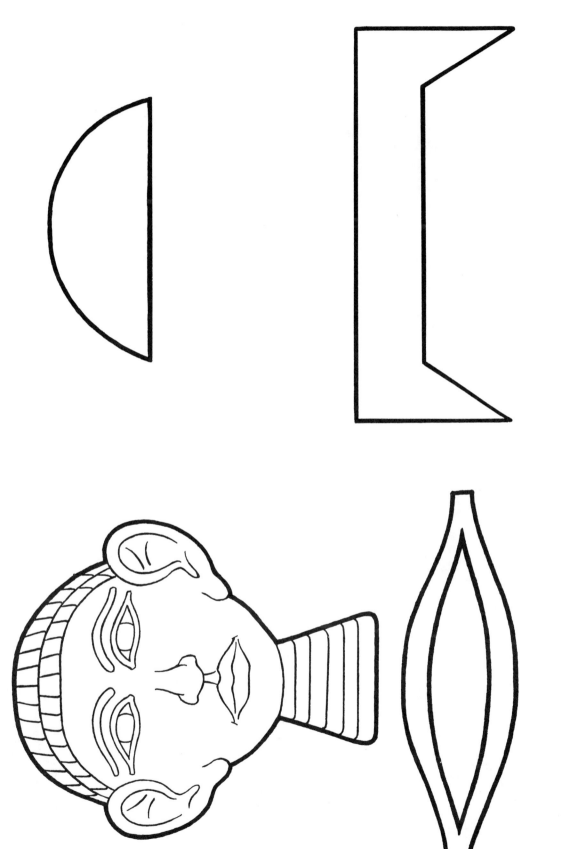

HR

Transliteration
ḤRT

Pronunciation
HERET

Meaning
SKY

Transliteration	Pronunciation	Meaning
ʿNḪT	ANKHET	GOAT

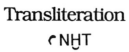

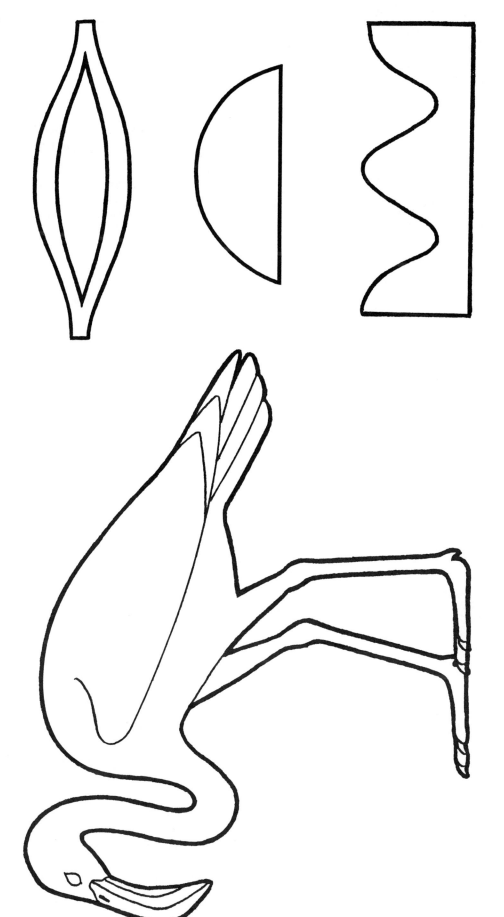

Transliteration
ˇ
DSRT

Pronunciation
DESHERET

Meaning
DESERT

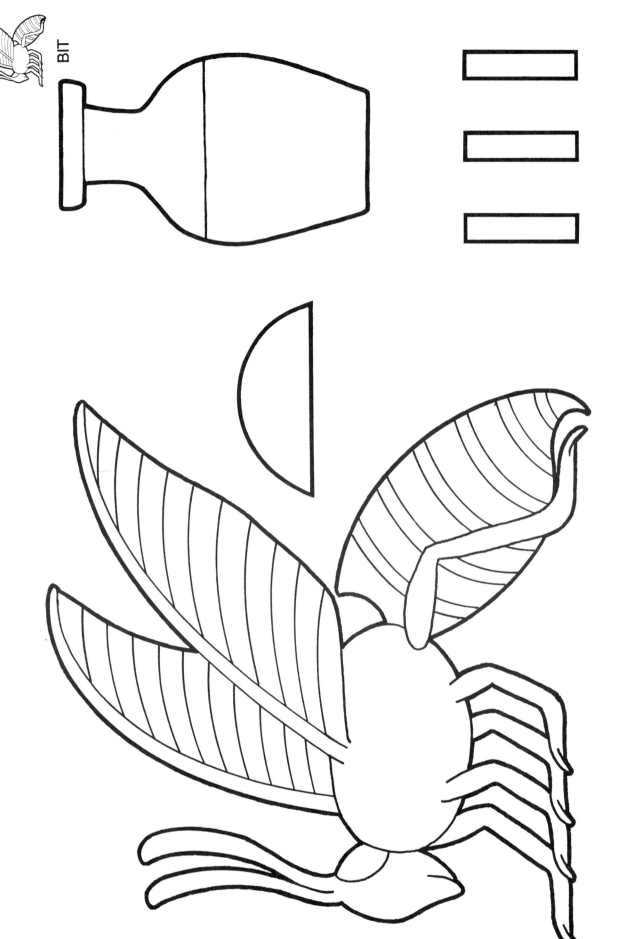

BIT

Transliteration

BIT

Pronunciation

BIT

Meaning

HONEY

MT
MWT

Meaning MOTHER

Pronunciation MUT

Transliteration MWT

HPR

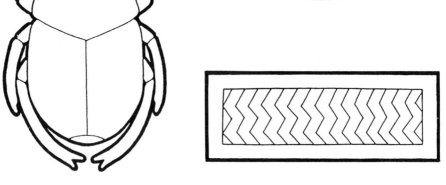

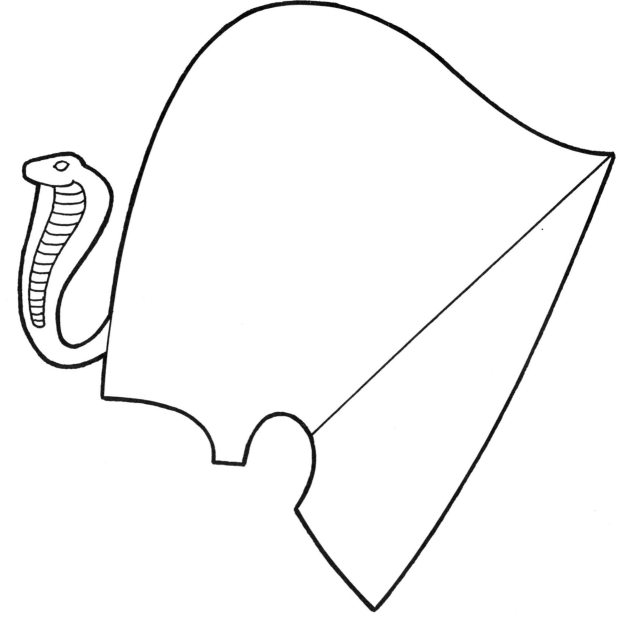

Transliteration	Pronunciation	Meaning
ḪPRŠ	KHEPERESH	BLUE CROWN